Where to Watch Wildlife in Devon

Robert Hesketh

Bossiney Books

First published 2011 by Bossiney Books Ltd
33 Queens Drive, Ilkley LS29 9QW
www.bossineybooks.com

ISBN 978-1906474-31-7

All photographs are by the author or from the publishers' own collection.
The map is by Graham Hallowell.

Printed in Great Britain by R Booth Ltd, Penryn

Spot the frog and the newt beneath the spawn in this small Dartmoor pond. When you're wildlife watching, there's often a lot more to see than immediately meets the eye...

The photograph on the title page shows a female gatekeeper butterfly

Whilst the information in this book was, to the best of our knowledge, accurate at the time of going to press, some changes may occur, for example to phone numbers or website addresses – and possibly to local government funding of visitor centres, free car parks, etc. We thought it best to include such information nonetheless, and hope you are not incovenienced by any changes which do occur.

Author's acknowledgements

My thanks to everyone who has helped towards this book in providing expert advice and observations, especially John Allan of the RSPB for his expertise on birds, John Randall for his help with butterflies and bugs, Phil Page of Devon Nature Walks, Andrew Cooper (author of *Secret Nature of Devon*) and Kevin and Anne Atkinson of Devon Badger Watch.

Introduction

Devon is a great place for wildlife watching, with a huge variety of animal and plant life. It has excellent nature reserves some of which are described in this book, with practical notes on how to find them, what there is to see and when to see it, together with information on facilities such as parking, toilets and refreshments.

From lowland heath to upland moor, saltmarsh and sea cliffs to rivers, lakes and woods, Devon provides a remarkable range of habitats. Whilst reserves give some of the best opportunities for wildlife watching, especially as wild creatures there are accustomed to seeing people, there are many other hotspots, notably on Dartmoor and Exmoor and along the coasts.

In fact wildlife recognises no man-made boundaries and may be encountered everywhere among Devon's 672,000ha (1.66 million acres). Most of the county is farmland, but surprisingly rich in wildlife compared with more intensively cultivated areas of Britain. In particular, Devon retains a large mileage of hedges, which support a huge variety of wildlife. Gardens also provide a rich habitat, particularly if owners plant trees and shrubs, feed birds, use organic methods and compost their waste.

We have not included in this book zoos or other venues with captive species, with the exception of two otter sanctuaries.

Whether you're wildlife watching from your kitchen window or visiting Devon's countryside, there's a lot more to see than immediately meets the eye, but the more you watch, the more you realise how and where to look. Wherever you watch, keeping as quiet and still as possible will boost your chances of success. Equally, avoid bright clothing and sudden movements and keep downwind of animals.

Please follow the Country Code. Picking up litter, guarding against fire and keeping dogs under control – particularly in the nesting season – all make a real difference to conserving wildlife.

Birds

With its wide diversity of habitats, Devon has birdwatching opportunities all through the seasons. Whilst the dawn chorus reaches its peak in May and June, the early spring, before the leaves appear, is best for seeing nesting and woodland birds at sites such as Yarner Wood (page 29) and Andrew's Wood (page 24) as they display and sing to establish territory and attract mates.

Curlews on the Otter estuary in December. Identified by their distinctive cries and very long, down-curved bills, these waders are noticeably larger than whimbrels and godwits

Turnstones feeding opportunistically on Brixham Quay. Shores are the natural habitat of these attractive small waders. The hide at Dawlish Warren (page 16) and Starcross on the Exe are good places to see them

Headlands on both south and north coasts, such as Prawle Point (page 23) and Hartland Point (page 32), are focal points for migrating birds. Mid- to late April is usually the peak for spring migrations and mid- to late September the height of autumn migrations.

The county provides shelter, rich feeding and a mild winter climate to huge numbers of overwintering birds. At Dawlish Warren (page 16) and Slapton Ley (page 22) and on Devon's estuaries, especially the Exe (pages 10-11 and 14-15), winter is a time for spectacular birdwatching, both in numbers and variety.

Butterflies

The great majority of Britain's 59 listed butterfly species can be seen in Devon between April and October in a variety of habitats. Woodland

A pair of silver-washed fritillaries mating

glades, flower-rich meadows, verges and heathland present some of the best opportunities. Devon is particularly good for fritillaries and noted sites include Bovey Valley Woodlands (page 29), Braunton Burrows (page 33) and Dunsford (page 28). Warm, humid, still summer days are ideal. Gardeners can help butterflies by growing a variety of nectar rich flowers through the seasons, along with food plants for caterpillars. Buddleia is a magnet for butterflies.

Badgers

The West Country has a dense badger population and badger setts (groups of large holes usually with extensive earth workings) are widespread through Devon, especially in woodland and in hedge-banks. Like other wild mammals including otters, foxes and deer, badgers are wary. Watching them requires patience and persistence. They are most likely seen at dusk or dawn, or heard at night. They are more active at these times, when there are fewer people (and their dogs) to disturb them, than in broad daylight. Devon Badger Watch (page 12) is a special opportunity to see wild badgers at close quarters.

Deer

All of Britain's eight deer species are basically forest animals. They will venture into open country to feed, but prefer to be close to dense cover. Although widespread through Devon, they favour well-wooded

Even if you don't see the deer themselves, you may see their slots (hoof-prints) or, as here, their droppings

areas, especially Exmoor (page 37) and Haldon (page 15). Look out for their slots (hoof prints) in soft earth. You may hear them occasionally or see them amid the trees if you are quiet and observant. Well camouflaged, they will often stand stock still and so go unnoticed. Deer can be seen year round, but they are least shy and the males most vociferous in the rut – October for red and fallow deer, July/August for roe deer. Deer are easier to spot once the leaves fall.

Otters

Otters hunt all Devon's major rivers and many of its minor ones. Surprisingly adaptable, resilient and unafraid of dogs, they even frequent Devon's towns and cities, including Exeter. Otters are largely nocturnal – early morning and late evening are the likeliest times to see them in the wild. The 'spraint' (droppings with a fishy odour) with which they mark their territories and their webbed five-clawed paw prints are distinctive.

Bats

All 16 British bat species live in Devon, a stronghold for these protected animals. Bats hibernate from October to April, often roosting in caves. Feeding on insects, they are most active on warm summer evenings and best seen over still water such as ponds, lakes and reservoirs or along woodland edges. Planting night-scented flowers, such as stocks, and erecting bat boxes will help them.

Seals

Atlantic (grey) seals are the most frequently seen around Devon's coasts. They breed from September to December and are often

This ocean sunfish was spotted off Combe Martin, from a Wildlife Coastal Cruise (see page 36). The sunfish is the world's heaviest bony fish, typically 1.8 m long and weighing around a tonne

very vocal at that time, when the majority of sightings are reported. Despite their size – males grow to over 2 metres and weigh well over 200 kg, the females average a little under 2 metres and a modest 155 kg – seals blend in to the background of rocks and sea, so scan both.

Dolphins and porpoises

Harbour porpoises and bottle-nosed dolphins are the cetacean species most often seen around the Devon coast. Watching hotspots for them and for seals include Ilfracombe (page 35), Hartland Point (page 32) and Prawle Point (page 23).

Sharks

Sometimes reaching ten metres long and weighing up to seven tonnes, basking sharks are Britain's largest animal and regular visitors to Devon's waters.

Rockpooling

There are great opportunities for rockpooling on many beaches, notably Ilfracombe Tunnels (page 35) and Wembury (page 24). Look *under* stones and seaweed, but please replace everything as you found it and return specimens promptly to the water. Take nets and a collecting bucket, and wear sturdy footwear with a good grip – rocks are uneven and slippery.

Eastern Devon

1 Axmouth and Lyme Undercliffs National Nature Reserve

This 304 ha reserve was created by a series of landslips. Stretching 11 km from Bindon Cliffs to the Dorset border on the outskirts of Lyme Regis, much of it is dense woodland, established by natural succession. The woods, one of Britain's finest 'wildernesses', are eerily quiet apart from birdsong and the murmur of insects, though there are areas of open grassland, wetland and scrub too, providing a diversity of habitats. The only access is via the Coast Path, Lyme Regis being the easiest point of entry.

What's to see? There are many species of woodland birds. Wildflowers and butterflies thrive in open areas.

When to see it? Visit in spring for wildflowers and woodland birds. The Undercliffs are a green jungle in summer – winter is ideal for studying the extraordinary geology.

Getting there Use Holmbush car park, Lyme Regis, SY336920.

Facilities Parking (paying), toilets and café.

Access Follow the Coast Path westwards. Although the path is uneven, do not leave it – there are deep fissures and unstable ground.

2 Axe Estuary

What's to see? Like the Exe and Otter estuaries, the Axe estuary attracts large numbers and many species of waders and wildfowl, especially at low tide. More birds flock on the neighbouring Axe and Seaton marshes. Otters are often seen from the bird hides. Spotting 40 bird species is not unusual on the Seaton Tramway's excellent guided birdwatching trips (February-November, 01297 20375).

When to see it? Although winter is best for waders and wildfowl, there's wildlife year round. Swallows, swifts and martins feed over the marsh in summer, as do bats. Woodland birds thrive in trees fringing the reserves.

Getting there/access Follow the Seaton Tramway signs. To view the Axe from the east, park by Axe Bridge or Axmouth.

Facilities Car park (paying) and toilets at the tram station; bird hides at Colyford Common and Seaton Marsh.

3 Aylesbeare Common SSSI

What's to see? As well as Dartford warblers, stonechats, linnets, pipits and many woodland birds, over 30 butterfly species are regularly

Birds landing on Axe Marsh. This photograph was taken from the Seaton tram, effectively a mobile birdwatching platform running alongside the Axe estuary

Right: Aylesbeare Common. The mires are a great place to see dragonflies and damselflies

recorded. Visit the mires to see dragonflies, damselflies and insectivorous plants including sundew. Roe deer, rabbits and badgers inhabit the woodland areas; adder, grass snake, smooth snake, slow worm and common lizard are found on the heath.

When to see it? Spring is the time for frog spawn and newly arrived migrant birds. Butterflies and dragonflies, sunbathing lizards, slow worms and snakes need summer warmth. Nightjars are heard and bats seen at dusk on summer evenings. The heather blooms in late summer and early autumn. Fieldfares and redwings are among the winter migrants.

Habitat protection Lowland heath like Aylesbeare is an increasingly rare habitat. It is carefully managed by RSPB to prevent invasive scrub, using grazing by cattle, bracken control and 'swaling' (controlled burning).

Getting there Use the free car park (SY057897), signed from the A3052 Exeter-Sidmouth road.

Access Two well signed trails of 1 km and 5 km.

4 Otter Estuary

What's to see? The estuary's 23 ha of tidal mudflats and saltmarsh provide rich feeding for many waders and wildfowl. Scan the reed beds, water meadows and trees for more species. Look out for shoals of grey mullet in summer.

When to see it? There is wildlife to see all year round, especially at low tide. Winter is best for birdwatching.

Getting there Start from Budleigh Salterton's Lime Kiln car park, SY074820.

Facilities Birdwatching platforms, bird hides, car park and toilets.

Access The 1 km path upriver from the car park is level and well-surfaced. Cross to the east bank to access the further bird hide via the Coast Path.

5 Bowling Green Marsh, Topsham

What's to see? The Exe estuary is the best place in Devon to see waders and wildfowl, in variety and in abundance. Select your time and place according to the tides. At low tide most birds are far out on the mud flats and best seen from a boat (see 'Bird cruises' page 15) or with binoculars from Topsham's Goat Walk (below) or Exminster/ Powderham Marshes (page 14).

High tide brings many birds onto the abundant grazing at Bowling Green Marsh, where the hide allows remarkably close views and bird-watchers have a regular programme, 'Showing People Birds', designed for beginners.

When to see it? The marsh is rewarding all year, but winter – when some 20,000 wetland birds visit the Exe estuary – is ideal.

Habitat protection At the time of writing, the RSPB was looking to create suitable habitat further up the Clyst for birds which will be displaced if global warming causes sea levels and tides to rise.

Getting there Follow Topsham's Fore Street south to the end of the Strand. Continue to the end of the bankside path (the Goat Walk). Turn left along the lane. Turn right at iron gates to a bird watching platform, or continue for 300m to the hide at SX972874.

Access The mainly level walk from Topsham is 1.5km (1 mile).

Facilities Car parks and toilets in Topsham. Birdwatching platform and hide. RSPB shop at Darts Farm near Topsham.

A view from the hide at Bowling Green Marsh

Wild badgers close up, courtesy of Devon Badger Watch

6 Rackenford and Knowstone Moors

A mixed habitat of wet grassland, bog, scrub and heath, the moors are the largest area of Culm grassland left in Devon (or anywhere else).

What's to see? Among 28 recorded butterfly species is the rare marsh fritillary. Birds include curlew, whinchat and stonechat, along with woodcock and snipe in winter. Red and roe deer are abundant, as are foxes and badgers. Culm supports a rich variety of wildflowers.

When to see it? Go in spring for wildflowers; summer for butterflies; autumn for deer watching.

Getting there Take the KNOWSTONE turning from the North Devon Link Road (A361), drive past the parking area (facilities), over the cattle grid and park by Knowstone Moor Cross.

For Rackenford Moor, take the ROSE ASH turning. Turn left past the parking area (facilities). Turn left at Hares Down Cross, over the A361. Park on the right.

Facilities Parking. Toilets at A361 parking areas.

Access Surfaced paths lead to the heart of the moor. Visitors are free to explore further, but the ground is rough and very wet.

7 Devon Badger Watch, Stoodleigh near Tiverton

What's to see? An exceptionally good opportunity to watch wild badgers close up at eye level from a special woodland hide. The badger

clan here has become accustomed to lighting and human presence –
but they remain wary and care is needed not to spook them. Special
sessions are available both for photographers and for children.
When to see it? Mondays to Saturdays, late evenings April to October.
Booking essential, 01398 351506. www.devonbadgerwatch.co.uk
Getting there 8km north of Tiverton off the A396 Exe Valley Road.
Ask for full directions when booking.
Facilities Hide (with lighting and chairs), small visitor centre, toilets.
Access Via a field and a lit path with some steps.

8 Grand Western Canal, Tiverton

This is an 18km (11¼ mile) long Local Nature Reserve with a continuous foot/cycle path.
What's to see? Waterfowl, especially mallards, moorhens and swans,
are abundant and kingfishers not uncommon. Water and tree cover
attract many other birds. Wildflowers draw butterflies and dragonflies. Badgers, foxes and roe deer are seen, most often at dusk or dawn.
Otter spraint and tracks are regularly recorded.
When to see it? Year round. Go on summer evenings for bats and
martins, swifts and swallows.
Getting there Follow the signs to Canal Hill. Enquiries 01884 254072.
Facilities Parking (paying), disabled access, toilets, café and bar, tea
room and visitor centre (01884 253345).
Access Other access points with parking include Manley Bridge, Hal-
berton, Sampford Peverell, Westleigh and Lowdwells.

9 Exeter, Cricklepit Mill

The headquarters of Devon Wildlife Trust: it has helpful staff, and
leaflets and interactive computers explain Devon's diverse wildlife.
What's to see? The wildflower meadow is home to poppies, daisies,
cornflowers and nearly 100 other species – a riot of colour. Otters visit
the mill regularly at night. Watch them on screen.
When to see it? Cricklepit Mill is normally open 9-5, Mondays to
Fridays. Visit in spring and summer for the wildflower meadow.
Getting there From Western Way car park, follow the footpath down
to the Quay. Continue along Commercial Road to the Bishop Blaize
pub. Turn right.
Facilities Interactive computers, parking (paying) nearby.
Access Full disabled access.

Cricklepit Mill, headquarters of the Devon Wildlife Trust

Winter bird-watching cruises on the Exe Estuary include expert commentary on the many species and huge flocks seen. Remember to take warm clothing!

10 Exminster Marshes

This is a 100ha RSPB reserve on the western shore of the Exe. Watch carefully: even big birds such as Brent geese are surprisingly inconspicuous in this terrain – unless they stage a honking fly past!

What's to see? Many regionally rare wetland birds nest here in spring, including lapwing. Warblers and skylarks are summer highlights.

When to see it? Year round, but a winter's day just after high tide is ideal.

Getting there From the A379 roundabout take the lane opposite the Exminster turning. Continue past the Swan's Nest pub and right to the RSPB car park. Follow the footpath to Turf Hotel (1.8km), a great bird watching place. Continue 2.5km downriver to Powderham church (alternative parking) or upriver 2km to the Topsham foot ferry (seasonal). The bankside footpath continues 7km north to Exeter.

Facilities Parking; viewing platform at Powderham Marsh.

Access Birdwatching here means exploring sometimes muddy footpaths, preferably with a map. Basically unsuitable for disabled access.

11 Birdwatching cruises

These provide expert running commentary, and are another great way to see the Exe estuary in winter. Many people watching the same place means little is missed and many species identified. Departing from Starcross and Exmouth, boats cruise from Dawlish Warren to Topsham. Full cruises take 3-4 hours, mini-cruises 1½ hours. Times vary with the tides. Details from RSPB 01392 246083 or Stuart Line Cruises 01395 222144 (summer) or 01395 276693 (winter).

South Devon

12 Haldon Forest Park SSSI

What's to see? Roe and fallow deer roam Haldon Forest Park's 1400 ha (3500 acres) of mixed woodland and heath. It has a nationally important population of nightjars, 34 recorded species of moth and butterfly and many birds of prey, including buzzards, peregrines, kestrels, hobbies and goshawks.

When to see it? Visit on warm sunny days in summer for butterflies. Calm conditions with rising currents of warm air are ideal for visiting the Bird of Prey Viewpoint. Deer can be seen year-round. In general, the further you are from the car park and humans the better your chances of seeing wildlife, but many woodland birds can be seen around the car park and frogs spawn in the pond there. See www.forestry.gov.uk/haldonforestpark for special events such as the spring dawn chorus and the autumn fungus foray and deer rut.

Getting there Follow the signs from the A38 Devon Expressway to Haldon Gate car park, SX884849. There is alternative access and parking at Mamhead, SX921807; from the A380 take the Starcross road and turn first right: the car park is 1km (½ mile) further on.

Facilities Parking (paying), café, toilets, cycle hire, tables and benches.

Access Some 40km (25 miles) of off road trails give access for walkers and cyclists. Avoid getting lost by using the signed trails. Collect free trail leaflets at the Ranger's Office. Some trails wheelchair-accessible.

Oyster catchers at Dawlish Warren, which is a bird-watcher's dream, with great flocks of waders and wildfowl, including brent geese and dunlin on the estuarine mud

13 Dawlish Warren

What's to see? Dawlish Warren NNR is a birdwatcher's dream. A varied habitat, with trees, fresh water ponds and reed beds, the Warren supports a wide variety of woodland and freshwater birds. Seawatching can be very rewarding too. Rabbits are numerous. With over 600 recorded plant species, the Warren is second only to Braunton Burrows (page 33) as a haven for flora.

When to see it? There is birdwatching year round, but two hours either side of high tide in winter is ideal for waders and wildfowl. Dolphins are seen in summer, Atlantic seals throughout the year.

Getting there Use the car park by Dawlish Warren railway station.

Facilities Toilets and refreshments. The visitor centre has helpful staff and literature, plus displays on wildlife and geology.

Access Follow the fairly level sandy path from the car park to the visitor centre and on to the bird hide (1.25 km/3/4 mile). Parts of the Warren may be fenced off to aid conservation.

14 Decoy Country Park, Newton Abbot

What's to see? Decoy has 40 ha (100 acres) of ponds, woodland, streams, heath and fen, and a 5 ha (12 acre) lake with breeding mallard, coot and moorhen, swans, Canada geese and other waterfowl. Essentially a wetland, Decoy supports frogs, toads, newts and native fish, drawing cormorants and sometimes kingfisher. Buzzards, ravens, crows, jays and woodpeckers, plus smaller woodland birds such as warblers, finches and robins live at Decoy. Evidence of roe deer, badgers and foxes is often found in the woods.

When to see it? Year round.

Getting there Leave the A380 (Torquay-Exeter road) at Penn Inn for Newton Abbot. Turn first left as signed.

Facilities Parking (paying), small visitor centre, toilets, refreshments and play park.

Access The Lakeside Trail is a surfaced 1 km route; the Fen and Woodland Trails (2 km and 3 km) are more demanding, but less visited.

15 Stover Country Park

This is 47.5 ha (114 acres) of mixed woodland, heath and marsh. Easily accessible, with good facilities and wildlife interest through the year.

What's to see? Stover's centrepiece is its 4 ha (10 acre) lake, a haven for a wide variety of birds, especially winter wildfowl. Woodland birds are complemented by marsh birds. Stover is noted for butterflies and 24 dragonfly species. Squirrels abound; roe deer are often seen. Look out for snakes and frogs.

When to see it? Summer is the time for dragonflies and butterflies, autumn for fungi. Whilst waterfowl can be seen throughout the year, winter is best for numbers and variety. Spring is ideal for woodland birds – be sure to visit the aerial walkway, where many species can be seen close to, especially on the feeder. Squirrels will almost certainly be there too!

Getting there Stover is signed 500 m south of the A38 Drum Bridges roundabout on the A383 Newton Abbot road, SX 833750.

Facilities Parking (paying), nearby bus stop, information boards and maps, bird hides, leaflets; toilets and picnic area. The Nature Interpretation Centre has varied displays and two CCTV cameras, which visitors can zoom in on birds. For Stover's events programme call 01626 835236.

Access The level walk around the lake and the aerial walkway are wheelchair friendly. There are several other paths, including a link to the Templer Way Heritage Trail. This follows the Teign. Sand martins nest in the banks; kingfisher and otter are sometimes seen.

16 Dartmoor Otter Sanctuary, Buckfastleigh

Why an otter sanctuary? When wild otter numbers were very low in Britain, sanctuaries such as this and that at North Petherwin (page 31) bred and released animals. Today, the sanctuaries take in sick and injured otters with the aim of returning them to their life in the wild. The hard work has paid off: otters have made a remarkable comeback

An otter at the Dartmoor Otter Sanctuary. You would need to be very lucky to see one in the wild

in much of Britain since the 1990s, further helped by improved water quality and protected species status. All the same, opportunities for seeing otters in the wild are rare.

What's to see? Otters! European, North American and Asian otters are kept in sizeable enclosures with plenty of water to swim and play in. (On the same site you will find 'Buckfast Butterflies', with large and wonderfully vivid tropical species.)

When to see it? Otter feeding times (normally 11.30 and 2pm) are especially lively: watching the otters swimming underwater in the glass tank is unforgettable. Normally open daily April-October, with limited winter opening. (Check on 01364 642916.)

Getting there Follow signs from the A38 at Buckfastleigh.

Facilities Free parking, toilets, café, picnic tables, bus stop and steam railway station.

Access Easy level access.

17 Paignton: Broadsands and Goodrington

What's to see? Both Goodrington and nearby Broadsands are easily accessible beaches with sea watching for cormorants, shags, grebes and oystercatchers. Behind Goodrington beach is Clennon Valley LNR, a reed-fringed lake with swans, coots, moorhens and various ducks. Scan the winter stubble fields behind Broadsands for cirl bunting. At the time of writing, the cirl bunting's only British habitat is the south Devon/south Cornwall coast, with hotspots including Broadsands, Berry Head, Prawle Point and Labrador Bay.

Goats are used for scrub control at Berry Head, which has a mix of grass, scrub and woodland. Its 60m high limestone cliffs support a rich diversity of fauna and flora

When to see it? Winter is best for birdwatching. As always, rock-pooling is best on an ebbing tide and ideal at the lowest spring tides. Goodrington's Seashore Centre (open in school holidays, 10am-4pm) hosts summer rockpool rambles.

Getting there Follow signs from the Paignton-Brixham road. Regular buses link Torquay, Paignton and Brixham.

Facilities Parking (paying), toilets and refreshments.

18 Berry Head NNR

What's to see? Among 200 bird species are the Channel coast's largest breeding colony of guillemot – regularly over 1000 birds. Other residents include cirl buntings, herring and black backed gulls, fulmars, kittiwakes and peregrines. Harbour porpoises, bottle nosed dolphins and basking sharks are often sighted. Some 500 species of lime-loving flowering plants, notably orchids, and 28 species of butterfly have been recorded. See bats roosting in the caves on the visitor centre's web cam.

When to see it? Year round, but early/mid-May is the best for nesting guillemots and spring flowers. To see migrating birds visit in the second half of April and in September.

Getting there Signed from Higher Brixham, or take Breakwater Road from central Brixham.

Facilities Car park (paying), toilets and bird hide. Visitor centre and café (seasonal). Two mobility vehicles for hire.

Access Good network of footpaths, mainly level and well surfaced.

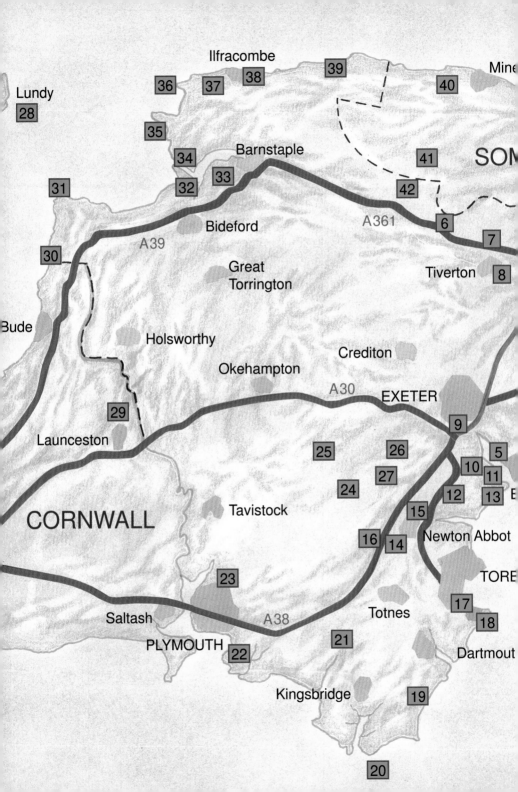

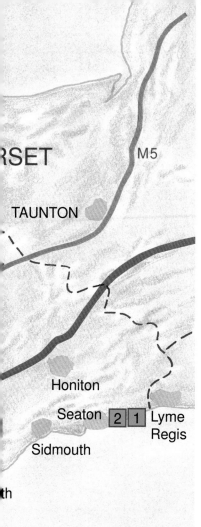

RSET

M5

TAUNTON

Honiton

Seaton 2 1 Lyme Regis

Sidmouth

Sites described in the text

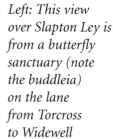

Left: This view over Slapton Ley is from a butterfly sanctuary (note the buddleia) on the lane from Torcross to Widewell

Lower photo: Prawle Point. A circular walk of 6km (4 miles) from East Prawle to Horseley Cove, Prawle Point and Gammon Head, returning to East Prawle via the Pig's Nose valley, provides a variety of birdwatching, including seabirds, heathland and woodland species

19 Slapton Ley

Covering 73ha (180 acres), the Ley is a haven for wildfowl. However, it is separated from the sea's fury only by a 4km/2½ mile long ridge of pebbles, making this remarkable ecosystem highly vulnerable to rising sea levels caused by global warming. If the sea breaks through, some freshwater species that thrive now would probably leave. Freshwater fish would die, but estuarine birds would thrive, as would salt-tolerant plants. Anyone interested in the local environment should visit Slapton Ley Field Centre (01548 580466), which offers wildlife, geology, ecology and conservation courses, all with local field work.
What's to see and when? Slapton Ley is renowned for birds. Spring

brings passage migrants, including thousands of house martins, sand martins, swifts and swallows. Large numbers of roach, rudd and perch spawn in April, attracting otters and pike: watch from Slapton Bridge, between the Lower and Higher Ley. Summer brings many butterflies and dragonflies; glow-worms light summer evenings. Migrating eels are seen in autumn at Torcross Weir, when up to 20,000 swallows and 2000 wagtails roost in Slapton's reed beds. This is dwarfed by the starling roost in December, estimated at 75,000 – a bonanza for peregrines and sparrowhawks. Winter wildfowl include gadwall, goldeneye, pochard, shoveller, tufted duck and wigeon. Scan the sea for grebe and divers.

Getting there A379 Dartmouth-Kingsbridge road.

Facilities Car parks (paying) at Torcross or Slapton Bridge, bird hide near Slapton Bridge, toilets, pubs in Torcross and Slapton.

Access A level footpath follows the north bank from Slapton Bridge, whilst the Coast Path (also mainly level) runs between the road and the east bank.

At Beesands, 4km south at SX819410, is Widdicombe Ley, a smaller version of Slapton Ley and another great place to watch birds, with its own hide.

20 Prawle Point

What's to see? Prawle Point is excellent for seals, dolphins and porpoises. Notable birds include cirl bunting, stonechats, wheatears and yellowhammers – all of which attract kestrels, buzzards and peregrines. Prawle is noted for migrating birds. Flocks of martins, swifts and swallows are especially impressive. Coastwatch staff frequently see wildlife from Prawle Point Station. Other duties permitting, they welcome visitors and share observations.

When to see it? Mid- to late April is usually the peak for spring bird migrations and mid- to late September the height of autumn migrations. Contact the RSPB for current information (see page 39). Marine mammals may be spotted at any time, but September to December is best for seals.

Getting there Follow the road through East Prawle to Prawle Point car park (National Trust) SX775355.

Facilities WC, café, pubs and shop in East Prawle.

Access The walk to Prawle Point is 500m.

21 Andrew's Wood

What's to see? There is a good range of woodland birds, including marsh tits, nuthatches and song thrushes. Snakes and lizards bask in sunny, open areas, where many flowering plants thrive, as well as butterflies and damselflies.

When to see it? Visit in spring to see woodland birds and bluebells, summer for flowering plants and insects and autumn for flowering heather.

Getting there The entrance is on a minor road north of Loddiswell at SX713520.

Facilities Parking (free), information board and leaflet box.

Access The trails are well defined. Despite duckboards, it can be wet and muddy in parts.

22 Wembury Beach

A magnet for wildlife, and the centre of the Voluntary Marine Conservation Area that stretches 6.5 km from Gara Point to Bovisand.

What's to see? This is the best place in Devon to learn about rockpool life – crabs, prawns, sea anemones, starfish, blennies, gobies, seaweeds and more besides. Wembury Marine Centre (01752 862538, admission free), run by Devon Wildlife Trust, offers interactive displays, aquaria and regular rockpool rambles. Shore and sea birds are plentiful too. Explore the Coast Path to see buzzards and kestrels, yellowhammers and cirl buntings.

When to see it? Low tide for rockpooling. Birdwatching throughout the year.

Getting there Follow the signs for WEMBURY from the A379, then the National Trust car park signs through Wembury (SX518486).

Facilities Parking, toilets, beach café/shop, marine centre.

Access Car park next to beach.

23 Plym Bridge Woods

What's to see? Peregrine falcons are the fastest creatures on earth, flying at over 190 km/h (120 mph) and swooping from great heights upon their prey. The National Trust maintains a 24-hour watch to protect a pair of peregrines from egg collectors and poisoners. The birds can be viewed in amazing detail through telescopes at Cann Viaduct from March to July (01752 341377 or www.plym-peregrines. co.uk for current news). They prey on the many other birds that

Andrew's Wood is sixty years old, and was established by natural generation. It has open areas of damp, grassy land, grazed by ponies

Many rocky beaches in Devon are good for rockpooling, but Wembury beach at low tide gives some of the best, as well as excellent birdwatching

inhabit the woods, home also to roe and fallow deer, badgers and foxes. The Plym provides a good habitat for herons, kingfishers and dippers, as well as trout and salmon, dragonflies and damselflies.

When to see it? Spring and early summer is best: the peregrines are nesting, fish are rising and the woods sporting anemones, primroses, wild garlic, foxgloves and bluebells. Go at dusk to see bats.

Getting there Plym Bridge is 6km east of Plymouth's city centre.

Facilities Parking (free) at Plym Bridge, SX523585.

Access Cann Viaduct (Peregrine Watch) is 2km north from Plym Bridge via the level and well surfaced cycleway, which continues through the woods and valley to Goodameavy. Rougher tracks lead deeper into the woods.

Dartmoor ponies with Widecombe in the background

Dartmoor

Dartmoor National Park's 954 km² (368 square miles) includes a wide variety of habitats and thus wildlife. Whilst heather, gorse and invasive bracken characterise the drier parts of the upland, mosses, cotton grass and reeds predominate on the extensive bogs. These are the source of many of Devon's rivers, including the Dart and the Teign, which flow through thickly wooded valleys rich in wildlife.

Skylarks and meadow pipits, along with ravens and buzzards, are the most memorable and frequently seen birds of the high moor, but it is the Dartmoor ponies that visitors remember best. Roaming the moor in semi-feral herds all year round, Dartmoors are one of Britain's nine native breeds. Spring and summer, when the long-legged foals follow their mothers closely, are the best times to see them. Each year, Dartmoor's pony herds are rounded up in the 'Drift' by their owners, some on horseback, and others on quad bikes. Traditionally, the Drift is in autumn, but sometimes there is also a drift in June. After sorting, some ponies are sold, but most released for another year.

Unlike the distinctly different Exmoor pony (page 37), Dartmoors have been extensively crossbred with Shetlands and other breeds, producing many piebald and skewbald animals. True Dartmoors are bay, brown, black, grey, chestnut or roan, and very hardy. They are short (12.2 hands – 1.27 m – or less) and stocky, with a thick mane and tail. Their coats are long and dense.

Please do not feed the ponies – it encourages them onto the roads – and do not pet them as they may bite or kick!

24 Dart Valley Nature Reserve

With 290 ha (696 acres) of moor and woods, the Dart Valley is Devon Wildlife Trust's largest reserve. There are several approaches, including a delightful walk from Venford Reservoir which skirts part of the upper fringe. The riverbank is accessed from New Bridge and Dartmeet.

What's to see? Look out for woodpeckers, willow and wood warblers and pied flycatchers in the woods, dippers and grey wagtails on the Dart. The reserve supports a range of butterflies. Otters hunt the Dart. The dense woodland, where mosses and lichens thrive in the clean, moist air, is ideal cover for deer.

When to see it? April is best for woodland birds, summer for butterflies, and rising trout. Go in November to see migrating salmon and sea trout – and glorious autumn colours (see photo below).

Getting there New Bridge and Dartmeet are on the Ashburton to Two Bridges road, at SX712708 and SX673733 respectively.

Facilities Free car parking, information board and toilets at New Bridge. Free parking and toilets at Dartmeet, as well as tearoom.

Access Unrestricted, but some of the terrain is very rough and there are few recognised paths. Walking between Dartmeet and New Bridge is a tough 13km. However, the first 1km downriver from Dartmeet is much easier, with a footpath; similarly the first 2km upriver from New Bridge or downriver towards Spitchwick are easy.

25 Fernworthy Reservoir, Dartmoor

What's to see? Fernworthy is an important staging post for migratory birds. Crossbills, redstarts, siskins and hobbies are among the more unusual birds seen in this woodland. At the north western side of the reservoir are two specially managed butterfly meadows, a haven for marsh fritillaries and marbled whites. Watch for brown trout.

When to see it? Rising trout are most often seen early morning and late evenings in summer. Go in summer for butterflies; April and September for migrating birds.

Getting there Follow signs from Chagford.

Facilities Free parking, toilets, picnic tables, two bird watching hides (one suitable for wheelchairs).

Access Follow the bankside footpath for 1km to the hides.

26 Dunsford Woods (from Steps Bridge)

What's to see? Famed for its abundant wild daffodils, this 57ha (137 acre) reserve has a great mixture of habitats and wildlife. The fast flowing Teign is ideal for trout and salmon – and otters. Wagtails, kingfishers and dippers thrive. Many fallow deer inhabit the woods. Woodland birds include woodpeckers, warblers, tits and pied fly-catchers. Devon Wildlife Trust keeps glades free of scrub, to encourage wildflowers and butterflies.

When to see it? Mid- to late March is usually best for daffodils. Bluebells follow in May. Early spring is ideal for woodland birds, summer for butterflies. October is best for deer and fungi, November for migrant trout and salmon.

Getting there Use the B3212 Moretonhampstead-Dunsford road or the B3344 Teign Valley Road.

Facilities Free car parks, bus stop, information board with map.

The Teign near Steps Bridge is famed for its daffodils. This photograph was taken at Steps Bridge, Dunsford Nature Reserve, home to a great variety of wildlife

Access A level 2.5 km (1 3/4 mile) bankside path leads from Steps Bridge. Beware of tree roots, cycles and horses. Please aid wildflower conservation by keeping to the path.

27 East Dartmoor National Nature Reserve

This consists of three adjacent wildlife sites: Yarner Wood, Trendlebere Down and Bovey Valley Woodlands. The woods support a rich diversity of lichens, mosses and ferns. There are also large areas of moorland and heath. Home to frogs and newts, the valley mires support water-loving plants: marsh orchid, bog asphodel and sundew.

What's to see? Butterflies such as graylings and fritillaries thrive on the heath, along with several birds, notably cuckoo, stonechat and Dartford warbler. Woodpeckers, nuthatches, tits, ravens and buzzards are often seen or heard. Look for signs of deer, badgers and foxes. Dippers and wagtails forage and otters hunt the river.

When to see it? Early spring for woodland birds. Trendlebere Down is noted for cuckoos. Dawn and dusk are best for mammals. Redwings and fieldfares are among visiting winter birds.

Getting there Use the Bovey Tracey-Manaton road.

Facilities Yarner Wood has a signed free car park (SX788789), toilets, information board, leaflets with maps, bird hide, field museum.

Trendlebere Down, with footpath access to Bovey Valley Woodlands, has two free car parks at SX783793 and SX773796.

Access Yarner Wood has two waymarked trails, 2.5 km and 3.25 km. Trendlebere Down and the Bovey Valley Woodlands are well served by footpaths.

Lundy's spectacular west coast: scan the cliffs and coastal heath for birds and the sea for seals, dolphins, porpoises and basking sharks

Marsland Mouth has a rich variety of habitats and wildlife, but requires energetic exploration on foot

Northern Devon

28 Lundy

Lundy is a granite island 20km off the North Devon coast and has remarkably rich flora and fauna. The seas around it are England's only statutory Marine Nature Reserve.

What's to see? Over 400 bird species have been recorded. Lundy is an important point for migrating birds. These include the now rare puffins which gave Lundy its Norse name. Seals, dolphins, porpoises and basking sharks are often seen, as are Soay sheep, goats, sika deer and Lundy ponies.

When to see it? Early summer, during the bird breeding season, is ideal.

Getting there Regular sailings go from Bideford and Ilfracombe (weather permitting) in summer, and helicopter flights from Hartland Point in winter. Day and period return tickets are available, plus a variety of accommodation and warden-led activities, including nature walks. Book on 01271 863636.

Facilities Pub, shop, toilets and accommodation.

Access Extensive access. Mixed terrain with paths.

29 Tamar Otter and Wildlife Centre, North Petherwin

Although just across the Cornish border, we've included it because, along with the Dartmoor Otter Sanctuary (page 17), it offers the best opportunities of seeing these fascinating animals at close quarters.

What's to see? As well as British and Asian short-clawed otters, there are fallow and muntjac deer, wallabies, Scottish wildcats, tawny, little, snowy and eagle owls, kestrels, waterfowl and peacocks.

When to see it? The centre is open daily in season (01566 785646). Otter feeding times are accompanied by informative talks at 12 and 3pm.

Getting there Signed off the B3254 Bude road 6km north of Launceston, at SX287894.

Facilities Shop, café, free parking, toilets.

Access Disabled access

30 Marsland Nature Reserve

A beautiful wooded valley leading down to the sea, with coastal heath, grass and glades. Located in a remote area by the Cornish border it takes some finding and must be explored on foot (take boots).

What's to see? There is a rich diversity of coastal and woodland birds. Wildflowers abound. Otters are frequently recorded. Butterflies thrive in the glades, dragonflies in the ponds.

When to see it? Spring is best for flowers, summer for butterflies.

Getting there Turn west off the A39 at Crimp, signed MORWENSTOW/ RIDING STABLES. Continue 3.5km to Shop. Turn right for GOOSEHAM. Turn left just before the stables. Continue past West Gooseham Farm. Turn right at the T-junction. Park carefully on the roadside 1km ahead, just past a sharp left hand bend. Take the path signed MARSLAND MOUTH, downhill through a gate to the information board/map.

Access The terrain is rough and muddy. Please keep to the paths.

31 Hartland Point

What's to see? Hartland Point is a landmark for migrating birds, as well as peregrines, ravens and buzzards. Seals, dolphins and porpoises are often seen.

When to see it? Go in spring or autumn for migratory birds. Marine mammals may be spotted through the year.

Getting there Hartland Point (not to be confused with Hartland Quay) is 5km beyond Hartland village: the car park is at SX235275.

Facilities Parking (paying), seasonal café, information boards.

Access It's a five minute walk on an uneven path up to the Hartland Point viewpoint.

32 Northam Burrows Country Park

625 acres (253ha) of saltmarsh, sand dunes and unimproved grassland grazed by ponies and sheep.

What's to see? Rabbits gave the Burrows their name. Badgers thrive there too. Wheatears and skylarks find a haven in the dunes. Visit the saltmarsh to see waders and ducks.

When to see it? Go in summer to hear skylarks and see maritime flowers. Winter is best for birdwatching on the saltmarsh.

Getting there Follow the signs from Northam Square, or take Pebbleridge Road from Westward Ho!

Facilities Parking, toilets and information centre.

Access Except for the golf course, the Burrows can easily be explored on foot. Follow the Coast Path from the Information Centre, between the golf course and the dunes.

33 Isley Marsh SSSI

An area of saltmarsh, tidal creeks and mudflats on the Taw/Torridge estuary. It is most easily accessed from Fremington Quay, itself a good place to watch waders and wildfowl.

What's to see? The estuary is an important feeding site for many birds, including oystercatchers, redshanks, golden plovers and spoon-bills; trees along the Tarka Trail attract a medley of woodland birds.

When to see it? Winter is best for ducks and waders. Go in spring and summer for shelducks and little egrets.

Getting there Turn off the B3223 at Fremington for FREMINGTON QUAY. Follow the Tarka Trail from the car park past the café and

Hartland Point, one of Devon's hotspots for seeing migrating birds. Note: the path to the rocky end of the Point is really difficult and cannot be recommended

Braunton Burrows. Its remarkably rich animal and plant life have earned it UNESCO Biosphere Reserve status

heritage centre. Cross the iron bridge and continue to Salt Pill Duck Ponds. Isley Marsh is another 1.5km (1 mile) along the Trail.
Facilities Free car park, picnic area, café/heritage centre.
Access Level access suitable for cycles and wheelchairs.

34 Braunton Burrows

A massive 978ha (2417 acre) dune system at the Taw/Torridge estuary.
What's to see? Skylarks, stonechats and whitethroats are among many birds seen at Braunton Burrows, which hold 33 species of butterfly and over 600 species of flowering plants. A large rabbit population attracts foxes, buzzards and kestrels. Watch waders and herons on Braunton Marsh and Swanpool Marsh behind the Burrows, where dragonflies and wetland plants thrive. Otters and barn owls are sometimes seen.

When to see it? Visit in spring and summer for flowers and butterflies, but the Burrows provide year-round interest, including resident birds, migrants and overwintering species. Seals are sometimes spotted at high tide, wading birds as the tide recedes.

Getting there The southern end of the Burrows is best for wildlife watching. From Braunton, take the toll road signed to Crow Point, across Braunton Marsh. Alternatively, park at Saunton Sands to explore the northern end of the Burrows. Swanpool Marsh Reserve is at the western end of Braunton off Moor Lane (SS473365).

Facilities Car parks at Crow Point (free at the end of the toll road) and Saunton Sands (paying). Toilets and refreshments at Saunton Sands.

Access The public is normally welcome on the Burrows, but part is used for military training. On rare occasions, red flags are flown and this area is closed for live firing. You may see soldiers and military vehicles – keep out of their way and don't touch any debris.

35 Baggy Point and Croyde Beach

What's to see? Baggy Point is a good watching place for marine mammals. Surrounding it is maritime heath, rich in wildflowers and butterflies. A rare and threatened habitat, it is characterised by gorse, heather and wildflowers such as primrose, bluebell and thrift. Further good examples on the north Devon coast include Morte Point (see below), Little and Great Hangman, Holdstone and Trentishoe Downs. Breeding birds include herring gull, fulmar, shag, kestrel, meadow and rock pipits, skylark, stonechat, wheatear and Dartford warbler. The dunes behind Croyde beach also have a variety of wildflowers, whilst the freshwater ponds contain a nationally important toad colony. Among the dunes are linnet, stonechat, reed bunting and sedge warbler. There is a rookery in the pines.

When to see it? Summer for wildflowers, butterflies, larks and pipits, but winter for sea birds. Visit the rockpools at low tide.

Getting there Use the National Trust car park or else park in Croyde.

Facilities Parking, toilets, cafés, pubs and shops.

Access The Baggy Point path (1.75km/1 mile) is wheelchair-friendly. Sandy paths lead to the beach and dunes.

36 Morte Point

Along with Baggy Point, this is one of Devon's finest maritime heaths.
What's to see? Many birds are seen, including wheatears, stonechats,

Lee Bay, an excellent beach for rock-pooling at low tide. Remember to look under the rocks, but replace them as you found them

nightjars, peregrines, gulls, cormorants and fulmars. Seals, dolphins and porpoises are often sighted. Sunfish, basking sharks and Portuguese man-of-war (an enormous jellyfish) are also reported.

When to see it? Year round, but Morte is most rewarding in summer, with its wildflowers and butterflies, lizards and adders.

Getting there Walk 1.75 km (1 mile) from Mortehoe car park.

Facilities Parking (paying), toilets, café, shops, heritage centre, restaurant and two pubs.

Access The paths are stony and sloped in parts.

37 Lee Bay

What's to see? Lee Bay's rockpools are easily accessible. Finds are similar to Ilfracombe Tunnels Beach (see below).

When to see it? Low tide – the rockpools are covered at high tide.

Getting there Use steep, narrow lanes from Mortehoe and Ilfracombe.

Facilities Parking (paying), café, pub, toilets.

Access Easy.

38 Ilfracombe

What's to see? Harbour porpoises and grey seals are regularly reported from Capstone Point and Tunnels Beaches. Search under the rocks and seaweed at Tunnels for crabs, whelks, periwinkles, anemones and dozens of other species. Scan the cliffs above for peregrine falcons.

When to see it? Capstone Point is rewarding year round. Tunnels Beaches are best at low tide.

Getting there and access Capstone Point is easily accessed from Ilfracombe's Landmark car park. Tunnels Beaches (modest entry charge) is nearby and signed.

Capstone Point, Ilfracombe: easily accessible, the Point provides good opportunities to watch sea birds and marine mammals

Feral goats have been associated with the Valley of Rocks, Lynton, for nearly 1000 years, but face an uncertain future

Facilities Parking (paying), toilets, cafés, pubs and restaurants.
Wildlife Coastal Cruises From Easter to October 1 1/2 hour trips are offered aboard the *Ilfracombe Princess* (01271 879727, Pier Kiosk). The 'East Cruise' follows the coast past Exmoor's hog-back cliffs, home for many nesting birds. Sightings of seals and dolphins are most likely on the 'West Cruise', past Morte Point into Woolacombe Bay.

39 The Valley of Rocks

This spectacularly beautiful valley west of Lynton is a mixed habitat supporting a variety of birds and 140 lichen species.
What's to see? Pied flycatcher, wood warbler and woodpecker can be seen in the woods, whilst guillemot and razorbill nest on the cliffs and the heathland supports whinchat, stonechat and wheatear. Look up

for peregrine and buzzard. The valley is grazed by Exmoor ponies and feral goats. Although their numbers have fluctuated, goats have lived here since at least AD 1086. The 'Friends of the Lynton Goats' support the animals, but their opponents point to the goats' marauding habits and campaign for culling. At the time of writing the goats' future was uncertain.

When to see it? Ponies and goats are most easily seen in winter. Kids are born in January.

Getting there A road runs through the valley and there are two car parks. However, the best way to appreciate the valley's remarkable geology and see its birds and the feral goats is on foot, using the level North Walk from Lynton or the more demanding path above the valley on the southern side.

Facilities Parking, toilets, picnic tables.

Access The North Walk is pushchair- and wheelchair-friendly.

Exmoor

Straddling the Devon/Somerset border, Exmoor National Park's 570 km^2 (220 square miles) of upland moor, heath, pasture and sea cliffs give plenty of scope for wildlife watching.

Exmoor ponies

Like Dartmoor ponies, Exmoors are native and roam as semi-feral livestock. Closer to the original wild stock than any other pony, their ancestors graced cave paintings in France and Spain, where our own ancestors rendered them in earthy ochres, umbers and blacks, strikingly similar to today's Exmoor ponies. Short and stocky, Exmoors are strong and hardy, with thick coats. You might see ponies anywhere on the open moor: beside the Lynton-Simonsbath road is a likely place.

Please do not feed or pet the ponies – it encourages them onto the roads and they may bite!

Red deer

Exmoor is unique in England in having kept a continuous red deer population since prehistory. Elsewhere, they have been reintroduced after being hunted to extinction.

Red deer are England's largest wild mammal. Mature males (stags) stand some 1.2m (4ft) at the shoulder and weigh around 295kg (650lb), of which 10 to 11kg (22-25lb) may be antler. Stags cast their

Red deer seen from a footpath near Molland

antlers late each April and then grow a new set, ready to contest with other stags for hinds in the autumn rut. The number of tines on a stag's antlers increases with maturity until age sets in and the stag starts 'going back'. The much more numerous females (hinds) do not grow antlers. They are smaller and slighter, but generally fleeter.

Red deer are widespread on and around Exmoor. Horner Woods, Tarr Steps and Molland Common are likely places – but they are shy, so don't expect to see them if there are crowds about.

Exmoor ponies

Wildlife calendar: month by month highlights

What's to be seen may vary by several weeks from year to year. Also, spring comes earlier and summer lasts longer in low-lying, sheltered sites than on cold and exposed ones, including Exmoor and Dartmoor.

January Snowdrops.

February Frog spawn, first primroses (Wray Valley, Lustleigh) and catkins.

March Wild daffodils (B3212 Teign Valley road and Steps Bridge). New Dartmoor and Exmoor pony foals. Winter birds depart.

April Return of summer birds, e.g. martins and swallows (swifts arrive in May), best seen at coastal migration points such as Hartland Point. Great increase in birdsong as birds mark territories and seek mates. First butterflies take wing. First cuckoo song. Hedgehogs, snakes, lizards and dormice appear after hibernation.

April to July – Peregrine Watch (page 24).

May Wildflowers, including bluebells. Dragonflies, damselflies and mayflies hatch. Dawn chorus reaches its peak during May and June.

June Long summer evenings are great for watching trout. Look out for bats and glow-worms as night falls.

July Roe deer in rut. The peak month for many butterflies.

August Heather in flower, whortleberries (Dartmoor, Exmoor, East Devon heaths).

September Bird migrations (best seen from coastal headlands). Seals breed through to December.

October Red and fallow deer rut. Autumn colours, mushrooms and other fungi.

November Sea trout and salmon running (try the Teign between Castle Drogo and Dogmarsh Bridge at SX 728898).

December First new lambs on well sheltered farms.

Useful contacts, websites and books

Devon Wildlife Trust (DWT) 01392 279244
www.devonwildlifetrust.org

Royal Society for the Protection of Birds (RSPB) 01392 432691
www.rspb.org.uk

British Naturalists Association 01536 262977
www.bna-naturalists.org

River dipping with the Devon Wildlife Trust: as with rockpooling, a fine mesh net will reveal a surprising variety of creatures

Devon Nature Walks 01392 211247
devonnaturewalks@btinternet.com

Dartmoor Nature Tours 0785 8421 148
www.dartmoornaturetours.co.uk

Wildlink (wildlife photography and walks) www.wildlink.org

British Dragonfly Society 01626 853393   www.dragonflysoc.org.uk

Devon Bat Group 01803 782218 and 01409 281178 www.dbg.me.uk

Devon Mammal Group www.devonmammalgroup.org

Book

Secret Nature of Devon, Andrew Cooper, Green Books, Dartington